Real Estate Investing Made Simple

Starting Your Own Property Management Business

Table of Contents

Chapter 1. Introduction

Welcome to our Special Report—Real Estate Investing Made Simple: Starting Your Own Property Management Business. In this user-friendly guide, we unravel the complexities of property management and break it down into digestible, actionable steps for aspiring entrepreneurs. You'll be invited to discover the lucrative world of real estate, where financial freedom isn't just a dream—it's your next big venture waiting to be realized. Right from the basics of scouting for properties, to managing tenants, to ensuring seamless operations, we've covered every corner. Get ready to take the leap and lay the cornerstone for your very own property management empire, with this comprehensive, yet cheerful guide, tailor-made for all the brave hearts daring to step into the arena of real estate investing. Buckle up, success is just a page turn away!

Chapter 2. Unraveling the Real Estate Market: An Overview

The real estate market is a labyrinth of opportunity, each corner bristling with promise and impending success. Yet, without a comprehensive understanding of its structure and functioning, it can be an ambitious venture to navigate successfully.

2.1. The Structure of the Real Estate Market

Understanding how the real estate market is structured is the first step towards mastering it. Unlike other markets, real estate markets aren't unified; they're fragmented into commercial, residential, industrial, and special purpose markets. Each submarket has its unique features, traits, properties, and regulations.

Different types of real estate include:

1. Residential Real Estate: This comprises both new construction and resale homes. The most common category, single-family homes, townhouses, condominiums, co-ops, duplexes, vacation homes, and residential lots fall under it.

2. Commercial Real Estate: This involves properties that generate income, such as shopping centers, medical and educational buildings, hotels, and offices. Apartment buildings are considered commercial even if they're used for residences, simply due to their business-generating nature.

3. Industrial Real Estate: This includes manufacturing properties and warehouses. These structures can be used for research,

production, storage, distribution of goods.

4. Land: This comprises vacant land, working farms, and ranches.

2.2. Economic Factors Affecting the Real Estate Market

The real estate market doesn't operate in a vacuum—it's intimately linked to the wider economy. Economic factors, including GDP growth rate, employment levels, manufacturing health, price of goods, inflation, and many more, can all have significant impacts on the real estate sector.

Some of the key economic indicators that you should understand and follow include unemployment rates, changes in gross domestic product (GDP), and consumer confidence indices, among others **(Table 1)**.

Table 1. Table 1 - Economic Indicators to Monitor in Real Estate

Economic Indicator	Description
Unemployment Rates	A high unemployment rate can signal a weak economy, suggesting a slowed real estate market.
GDP Changes	The Gross Domestic Product is a measure of economic activity within a country.
Consumer Confidence Indices	High consumer confidence can signal increased real estate transaction activity in the near future.

2.3. Legal Considerations

Real estate markets are also influenced by existing laws and regulations at both local and national levels. Zoning laws, tax laws, land use and environmental laws—all these and more can significantly impact the value of a property.

A strong knowledge of legal considerations is crucial. This is because property owners, investors, and real estate professionals are all liable for obeying these rules and requirements. Failure to do so can result in fines, penalties or legal actions.

2.4. Understanding Property Valuation

Property valuation is a critical skill for property management professionals. It involves determining the economic value of a real estate investment. Appraisers often determine this value by looking at the sales of similar properties in the area in a process called comparatives, or comps.

An understanding of property valuation can help investors to pinpoint the right price for buying or selling properties. In addition, lenders use property valuations to identify the amount they're willing to lend borrowers.

2.5. Demand, Supply and Their Impact Negotiation

The dynamics of supply and demand are pivotal in the real estate market. High demand and low supply often lead to price increase, whereas low demand and high supply tend to result in price reductions. Recognizing these patterns can present opportunities for savvy real estate professionals to negotiate effectively on property prices.

This knowledge, coupled with an understanding of the negotiation process itself, can enable property managers to secure advantageous terms. By learning the art of negotiation, the potential to increase your return on investment augments manifolds.

Unraveling the intricacies of the real estate market might seem daunting, but armed with the right tools and knowledge, the sky's the limit. Be aware that real estate isn't just about buildings or land, it's about finding places where people want to live or work. So, keep your finger on the pulse, watch, and respond to market trends, and who knows? Your property management empire might just be around the corner.

Chapter 3. Getting Started: Your Business Plan Blueprint

Having a well-crafted business plan is your very first step towards setting up a successful property management business. Your business plan is the blueprint of your venture—it defines what you intend to achieve and provides a road map of how you're going to get there. The following detailed sections guide you through the process of creating an exhaustive business plan for your property management endeavor.

3.1. Understanding Your Market

Before diving into the property management business, you must take time to understand the market you're targeting. Understanding your market goes beyond just a cursory glance at property listings. Start by determining your target audience. Are you focusing on residential or commercial properties? Luxury or budget properties?

Understanding your market should also involve understanding the dynamics of the real estate industry in your intended region. You need to be aware of market trends, demographic shifts, legislative changes, and economic indicators that affect your business.

Consider making use of resources such as market reports, demographic data from the national census, and market research reports from real estate industry bodies. This will give you market insights and help you to accurately analyze supply, demand, rental yields, and property occupancy rates.

Research your competition extensively - identify their strategies, strengths, and weaknesses. Understand the services they offer and their fee structures. Having this information will help you find a unique selling point for your business.

3.2. Define Your Services

Next, define precisely what services you will provide as a property management company. Some of the core services provided by property management companies include tenant acquisition, property maintenance, rent collection, and eviction handling.

However, you could also consider offering additional services for differentiation. These could include renovation management, financial advisory services, or concierge services for luxury properties. Defining your services clearly will help you position your business in the market and develop operational and pricing strategies.

3.3. Setting Up Your Business Structure

A crucial part of your business plan should be dedicated to defining your business structure. This means determining whether your business should be a sole proprietorship, a partnership, or a corporation. Each structure has its pros and cons and making the right decision could have far-reaching implications, including your liability in case of debts or lawsuits, your tax liabilities, and your ability to raise capital.

You may want to consult an attorney or a business advisor to understand the best structure for your business. While making this decision, remember to consider your future growth plans, possible risks, and financial goals.

3.4. Financial Planning

Any business plan is incomplete without a comprehensive financial plan. This should cover your start-up costs, operational costs, projected income, and potential profit.

Start-up costs will include things like acquiring office space, buying equipment, marketing costs, and regulatory fees. Operational costs should cover employee salaries, utilities, and maintenance costs. You will also need to factor in an allowance for unforeseen expenses.

In terms of income, you will need to have an idea of the rental yields you can expect from your properties, how much you will charge for your services, and when you expect to break even. Finally, you should also include a profit forecast to give potential investors an idea of the financial returns they can expect from your business.

Your financial plan should also include a pricing strategy for your services. This involves deciding whether you will charge a flat fee, a percentage of the rent earned, or a combination of both.

3.5. Marketing and Sales Strategy

Your business plan should define your marketing and branding strategies. How will you make your business known to your target audience? Will you use online marketing, direct mail, newspaper adverts, or other routes?

Your marketing strategy should align with your target market, your unique selling points, and your business objectives. The most effective strategies are usually a mix of online and offline methods, so consider leveraging multiple channels.

Your sales strategy should outline your approach to acquiring new clients, retaining existing ones, and maximizing revenue from each client. This may include things like offering referral bonuses, providing excellent customer service, or offering discounts for long-term contracts.

3.6. Operational Plan

This plan should detail the processes and resources you will use to deliver your services. It should cover things like how you will source properties, how you will handle tenants, and how you will do maintenance. You should also detail the teams you need, their work schedules, any external vendors you will need, and any software or systems you will use to automate tasks.

In conclusion, starting a property management business isn't just about having properties to manage—it's about planning carefully, understanding your market, working hard, and always staying focused on your goals. If you can do this, you stand a great chance of succeeding in this rewarding sector of the real estate industry.

Chapter 4. Scouting 101: Navigating the Property Landscape

For any aspiring property management entrepreneur, the journey begins with understanding the art of scouting or searching for potential investment properties. This is a critical first step that forms the basis for your entire operation. Without the right property, you can't implement the most strategic of plans or the best business models. Here is everything you need to know:

4.1. Understanding Your Investment Goals

A meaningful scouting venture begins with clarity on your investment goals. Are you looking for a steady source of rental income or quick gains through flipping properties (buying, improving, and selling properties)? Maybe you are interested in long-term wealth generation? Different objectives mandate different kinds of properties. For instance, rental property investors usually opt for properties in thriving rental markets where demand is high, while flippers prefer distressed properties they can renovate and sell for a higher price.

4.2. Choosing the Right Location

Location, Location, Location—they say it three times for a reason. It's an aspect you can't change once you invest, unlike the property's physical condition or rental price. Consider factors like population growth, economic health, job opportunities, school ratings, and amenities like parks and shopping centers. Real Estate analytics report that neighborhoods with a low crime rate, proximity to good schools, and good connectivity are often preferred by most tenants.

4.3. Analyzing the Real Estate Market

An astute investor is often a market-savvy investor. You need to gauge the market trends— understanding whether it's a buyer's market (more houses than buyers, prices drop) or seller's market (more buyers than houses, prices hike). It helps steer your negotiation. Use data from multiple sources, consult with local realtors and property managers, and discuss with area residents for their perspective. Notable market indicators include the average house price, average rent, and the vacancy rate.

4.4. Evaluating the Financial Feasibility

In the end, it boils down to numbers. Calculate the potential return on investment by considering the property's purchase price, the cost of any required renovations, potential rental income, and your operating expenses. Tools like the 1% Rule (monthly rent should be at least 1% of the property's purchase price) and the 50% Rule (half of your income will likely be spent on expenses, not counting mortgage payment) can aid your analysis.

4.5. Scouting Online

Internet scouting has opened new doors for real estate investment. Online platforms offer large databases of listed properties with details about price, location, condition, and seller information. Insider's tip: Use Google Earth to understand a property's locale without actually visiting.

4.6. Conducting Physical Inspections

Regardless of how good an online listing looks, never skip an in-person visit. Inspect for structural issues, pest problems, or any needed repairs. Hire a professional inspector if necessary. Pay keen attention to the condition of roof, foundations, HVAC system, electrical and plumbing systems, and look out for signs of water damage or mold.

4.7. Making the Purchase

Once you've found a potentially profitable property, it's time to negotiate a deal. If you're not confident of your negotiation skills, consider hiring a trusted real estate agent. Remember to leave some room in your budget for unexpected costs that can crop up during property acquisition.

4.8. Building a Network

Networking is paramount in the real estate business. Nurturing relationships with fellow investors, real estate agents, and other industry professionals can lead to fruitful partnerships and collective growth. They can provide crucial insider information or support in times of need.

Remember, numerous variables can affect a property's potential for profit — from broad economic factors to neighborhood-specific trends. Building a base of knowledge across all these areas and using that information to steer your investments can lead to impressive returns over the long term. With patience and grit, along with continuous learning and adaptability, you can surely navigate the choppy waters of real estate investing and steer your ship to the land of capital gains.

Chapter 5. Financial Foundations: Preparing for Your Investment

Property management and real estate investing can be complex arenas to enter, but with the proper foundation in finance, it can be substantially demystified. This chapter lays out the financial groundwork necessary for your successful entry into this rewarding field. Let's start.

5.1. Stabilizing Your Personal Finances

Your first step even before considering investing in a property is to ensure your personal finances are solid. The fundamental principles include having an emergency fund (enough to cover 3-6 months of living expenses), being nearly or entirely free of high-interest debt, and having a stable income. You might encounter situations where available cash is needed promptly, like maintenance emergencies or legal issues. Therefore, having both a safety net and a significant amount of available cash or credit is vital.

5.2. Understanding Real Estate Investment

Real estate investment is not a get-rich-quick scheme. It requires time, effort, and money to be successful, and there will be periods where it seems like nothing is going right. But given patience and diligence, real estate can be a highly profitable engagement.

Remember, investing in real estate is, fundamentally, an investment in a physical asset. This property has financial implications, including upkeep, property taxes, insurance, and potentially mortgage payments. Being prepared for these financial obligations is key to maintaining profitability and avoiding financial pitfalls.

5.3. Crunching The Numbers

A significant part of owning a property management business revolves around understanding the numbers. You should be able to calculate the potential return on investment (ROI), the capitalization rate, the cash flow, and the cost of managing the property (including maintenance, mortgage payments, insurance, and unexpected incidents).

One should also understand the concept of leverage, i.e., using other people's money to fund your investment. While loans increase your buying power and can accelerate your investment growth, these should be handled sensibly as they can also magnify your losses.

5.4. Budgeting For Property Management

Running a property management business comes with its own set of expenses. Hence it is necessary to incorporate these costs into your initial budget. These expenses might span across advertising, property refurbishing, regular maintenance, staffing, and potential legal fees.

The rule of thumb here, especially for beginning investors, is to overestimate your expenses and underestimate your income. This approach develops a safety margin that is helpful in coping with unexpected situations.

5.5. Understanding Financing Options

There are many ways to finance real estate purchases, including bank loans, hard money lenders, private lenders, or partnerships. Understanding the pros and cons of each approach is crucial for your financial understanding and decision-making process.

For example, while bank loans can offer low interest rates, they typically require strong credit scores and involve a lengthy approval process. On the other hand, hard money lenders or private lenders might provide funds more readily but at a higher cost.

5.6. Tax Implications

Lastly, understanding and planning for the tax implications of real estate investment is crucial. Depreciation, mortgage interest deductions, and business expense deductions can offer significant tax benefits. However, rental income is taxable, and selling properties can potentially incur capital gains tax.

Seek advice from a tax professional familiar with real estate investment, and learn about possible legal structures, like Limited Liability Companies (LLCs) or Limited Partnerships (LPs), that can offer further tax advantages.

5.7. Building Your Financial Team

In conclusion, you are not alone in this venture. Build a trustworthy financial team, including an accountant, attorney, and a real estate savvy banker or mortgage broker. They are invaluable resources in your journey, providing advice, keeping you compliant with local and state laws, and helping you manage the financial aspects of your property management venture.

Embarking on a property management business can feel like a steep climb, but with a stable financial foundation, the journey becomes manageable and rewarding. By comprehending and implementing the financial foundations laid out in this chapter, aspiring real estate entrepreneurs can prepare for their exciting investment journey.

Chapter 6. Due Diligence: Property Evaluation and Risk Management

Getting into the real estate business can be thrilling, and it's easy be swept away by the excitement of a promising property on the surface. But the real determinant of success is mastering the art and science of due diligence. The foundation of a profitable property management business is the ability to accurately assess properties and effectively manage risks. So, let's delve deep into the due diligence procedure with a wide yet detailed lens, from property evaluation to risk management.

6.1. Property Evaluation

The evaluation of a property is crucial to understanding its current value, future prospects, and potential risks. This can be broken down into multiple parts, including the physical characteristics of the property, location, and financial evaluation.

1. **Physical Evaluation**: The inspection should cover every inch of the property to discern the level of maintenance required. Check for structural integrity, condition of the building systems (like heating, cooling, electrical, and plumbing), the quality of finishes, and the layout of the property. You should also consider hiring a professional inspector to discover issues not obvious to the untrained eye.

2. **Location Evaluation**: A property's geographical location immensely affects its attractiveness to renters and therefore its profitability. Is it in an area with desirable amenities, such as schools, shopping centers, hospitals, and transportation options? What's the neighborhood crime rate? Look also at the

demographic trends to predict future demand.

3. **Financial Evaluation**: The potential profitability of a property lies not only in its rental income but also its costs. Do thorough research on the property's past, current and projected rental income, operating costs, financing costs, and property taxes.

6.2. Risk Management

Once you've gathered all the necessary information through property evaluation, it's time to tackle the next crucial pillar of due diligence—risk management.

1. **Identifying Risks**: The first step in risk management is identifying potential risks. These could be financial, such as unanticipated maintenance costs, unexpected vacancies, or sudden market changes that impact rent. They could also be legal risks like zoning laws, rent control regulations, and tenant rights. Also consider environmental risks such as natural disasters.

2. **Assessing Risks**: After identifying potential risks, it's necessary to assess their possible implications. An assessment will involve projecting the impact of each risk on your property's profitability and determining the likelihood of its occurrence.

3. **Mitigating Risks**: The final and most crucial step is planning how you will mitigate these risks. Insurance can be a lifeline for many types of risks. Other risk mitigation strategies could involve diversifying your property portfolio, planning a maintenance schedule, or even simply walking away from a property if the risks outweigh the potential income.

Let's not forget about the importance of maintaining proper documentation throughout the entire due diligence process. A Property Evaluation Checklist and a Risk Management Plan are two tools that every property management business owner should have in their toolbox. Remember, in real estate, the winners aren't those who find the most properties but those who find the best ones.

By this point, the idea of Due Diligence might seem overwhelming, but it is imperative for the long-term success of your property management business. Take your time and cultivate the ability to scrutinize and analyze, thinking three steps ahead. Lay your foundation right, and the empire of your dreams will stand tall on it.

Chapter 7. Mastering Tenant Management: The Art of Building Relationships

Tenant management is more than just filling vacancies and collecting rent—it's about forging strong, lasting relationships with your tenants. These relationships can mark the difference between a vacant property and a cash-flowing investment, so investing time and energy into fostering them is paramount.

7.1. Understanding Your Tenants

The first step in mastering tenant management is understanding who your tenants are. This may sound straightforward, but in reality, it goes beyond knowing their names and employment status. You must strive to tap into their needs, aspirations, attitudes, and behaviors. Grasping these dynamics will put you on strong footing to meet and exceed their expectations.

What are the predominant demographics? Are they young professionals, families, or senior citizens? Each group has unique needs. Young professionals could prefer close proximity to nightlife and fast internet connections, families could be more concerned about school districts and safety, and senior citizens may value easy access to healthcare facilities and minimal stairs. Knowledge of your tenants will guide you in shaping the offerings of your property management business.

7.2. Effective Communication

With an understanding of your tenants, you can tailor your communication strategies to fit them. But remember, effective communication is a two-way street—it's not just about delivering your message effectively, but also about listening and responding appropriately.

- Be proactive: Don't wait for problems to arise before communicating with your tenants. Regularly scheduled updates, newsletters, or simple check-ins can reassure your tenants that you're invested in their welfare.

- Be clear: Keep your messages simple, straight to the point and jargon-free. You want your information to be understood, not misinterpreted.

- Be responsive: Respond to queries and concerns promptly. Leaving issues unattended can seriously damage your reputation.

Communication also plays an integral role during conflict resolution. When disputes arise, staying calm and composed, listening empathetically, and offering reasonable solutions can turn a potential crisis into an opportunity for relationship-building.

7.3. Tenant Onboarding

The tenant onboarding process is the first real opportunity to set the tone for your relationship. Consider developing a detailed 'welcome package' for new tenants. This can include a copy of the lease agreement, contact information, instructions on how to pay rent and request maintenance, and any other tenant-specific information. Remember, a positive onboarding experience can pave the way for a strong long-term relationship.

7.4. Regular Inspections and Maintenance

Regular property inspections and timely maintenance are essential for tenant satisfaction and retention. You need to ensure that the property remains in good repair and any problems are promptly addressed. This not only increases tenant satisfaction but also help maintain the value of your investment.

Here are some key points to remember about inspections and maintenance:

- Periodic inspections: Schedule routine inspections, and inform your tenants well in advance.
- Preventive maintenance: It's cheaper and more convenient to fix potential issues early than dealing with the fallout of major repairs.
- Quick responses: When tenants issue a repair request, ensure you respond promptly and follow up to ensure the problem has been solved to their satisfaction.

7.5. Appreciating and Rewarding Loyalty

Lastly, showing appreciation to your tenants can go a long way in building loyalty. Simple gestures like sending a holiday card or acknowledging a tenant's birthday can make them feel valued. You might also consider implementing a tenant referral program, which can contribute to both tenant satisfaction and business growth.

7.6. Summing Up

Mastering tenant management is an art—one that entails understanding tenants' needs, communicating effectively, strategic onboarding, regular inspections, maintenance, and showing appreciation. Following these steps will build positive relationships, making your property management business not only financially successful but also personally rewarding. Remember: Relationships are the foundation on which strong businesses are built. Build yours wisely and watch your property management empire flourish.

Chapter 8. Under the Hood: Day-to-Day Operations

Opening a property management business is akin to peeling an onion: there are several layers of responsibilities, each needing its attention and expertise. Equipping yourself with comprehensive understanding is what differentiates a successful entrepreneur from an average one. In this chapter, we will embark on a journey, delving deep into the day-to-day operations that keep any property management business running effortlessly.

8.1. Understanding Your Tasks

As a property manager, your responsibilities are vast and diverse. Major tasks can be classified into three main categories: tenant management, property maintenance, and business operations.

- Tenant Management: Your first and foremost responsibility is to manage your tenants. This involves everything from finding and screening potential tenants to ensure they are reliable and will take care of the property, to setting and collecting rent, maintaining a strong landlord-tenant relationship and managing any issues or disputes that arise.

- Property Maintenance: Regular maintenance and repairs are a part of every property management business. This includes routine upkeep such as landscaping and cleaning, as well as handling any emergency repairs or improvements. Having a list of reliable contractors at your disposal is a huge asset in this regard.

- Business Operations: Lastly, you are running a business, and there are tasks related to this aspect as well. Managing financials, marketing properties, complying with local and federal laws, etc., fall under this category. Understanding each of these tasks and how you approach them sets the tone for your daily operations.

8.2. Tenant Management

Let's delve deeper into each of these categories, starting with tenant management.

Marketing your property effectively is the first step in tenant management. You need to get the word out about the properties you're managing, utilizing both online and offline channels. Online listing services, social media, and your own website are great places to start. Include high-quality images and detailed property descriptions to attract potential tenants.

Next, screening prospective tenants is crucial: this involves checking their credit, income, rental history, as well as conducting interviews. This process reduces the risk of leasing to unreliable or problematic tenants.

Rent collection is another critical task. Establish clear policies for when rent is due, how it can be paid, and what the late fees are. This can help you avoid common rent-related issues later on.

8.3. Property Maintenance

Now, let's shift gears and talk about property maintenance.

Routine maintenance tasks like lawn care, power-washing exteriors, servicing HVAC systems, and pest control must be regularly scheduled to keep the property in preservable condition.

Handling repairs and renovations is also part of this role. You need to be prepared to manage everything from minor repairs like a leaking faucet, to large-scale projects such as roof replacement or installing a new HVAC system. Maintaining a network of trusted contractors can be a lifesaver when it comes to timely and efficient repairs.

Plus, make sure you carry out regular property inspections. These can help identify potential issues before they become major headaches and show your tenants that you are proactive about maintenance.

8.4. Navigating Business Operations

Finally, let's discuss the ins and outs of running the business side of a property management company.

This involves managing finances meticulously. You'll need to have systems in place for collecting rent, paying bills, taxes, maintaining insurance coverage, and paying any employees or contractors. Plus, you should regularly analyze financial statements to monitor your company's fiscal health.

Marketing can't be emphasized enough. Aside from attracting tenants, it also promotes your business to potential partners and clients. Create a recognizable brand, maintain an engaging online presence, and be responsive to customer feedback.

Lastly, you must ensure that your company stays in compliance with all local, state, and federal property laws. This includes things like fair housing laws, eviction procedures, and safety regulations.

As a property management entrepreneur, you're constantly juggling multiple tasks. This chapter has provided an overview of what a typical day might look like. Remember, no two days are the same in property management. But with preparation and understanding, even the most hectic days can be navigated with ease and success. As the old saying goes, "The secret of your future is hidden in your daily routine." Make it an effective one, and your property management empire will surely thrive.

Chapter 9. Legal Avenues: Policies, Licenses and Regulatory Compliance

In the labyrinthine world of real estate investment and property management, it's critical to recognize and navigate the legal avenues proficiently. Before you begin scouting for properties or vetting potential clients, you'll need a grounded understanding of key policies, rules, and regulations. Equally important is ensuring you have the requisite licenses and have complied with the regulatory statutes governing property management in your area. Consequently, this chapter will lay out these legal parameters in a detailed yet understandable format, empowering you to move forward with confidence and integrity within the property management sector.

9.1. Licenses and Certifications

Most states in the US require property managers to carry a real estate broker's license, or to work under someone who does. While each state has different requirements, most necessitate that the candidate be over the age of 18 or 19, have a high school diploma or equivalent, and successfully complete a specific number of hours in real estate courses.

In addition to municipal or state requirements, a few professional certifications can not only lend credibility to your business but also enhance your knowledge and skills. Noteworthy amongst these are Certified Property Manager (CPM) from the Institute of Real Estate Management (IREM), Residential Management Professional (RMP) from the National Association of Residential Property Managers (NARPM), and Certified Apartment Manager (CAM) from the National Apartment Association (NAA).

Some states also mandate functional licenses for businesses involved in servicing property, like pest control, repair, renovation, and landscaping. Make sure you investigate these requirements thoroughly before operationalizing your property management business.

9.2. Understanding and Interpreting Policies and Regulations

Every state has its own legislation related to rental properties and property management. Usually, these laws establish the rights and responsibilities of landlords and tenants. They address issues of privacy, security deposits, lease requirements, eviction protocols, and property maintenance, amongst other things.

Key federal laws covering property management range from Fair Housing Laws that prohibit discrimination against tenants, to the Americans with Disabilities Act (ADA) that requires reasonable accommodations for individuals with disabilities.

It's important to comprehend your obligations under these laws and, at the same time, ensure your renters understand their responsibilities. This will help you manage your properties more effectively, reducing the risk of legal issues arising down the line.

9.3. Embracing Compliance

Regulatory compliance is not just about avoiding fines, penalties, or potential lawsuits. It is a crucial foundation for ensuring your property management business operates with the utmost integrity. Developing an excellent working relationship with local health, zoning, and emergency departments allows your business to have plans in place for resolving any issues which may arise, further reinforcing operating efficiency and credibility.

Introduce a systematic approach to ensure periodic inspection of properties to confirm they adhere to health and safety codes. Maintain robust documentation outlining property conditions, tenant interactions, and inspections, which will be instrumental in resolving disputes or demonstrating due diligence if required.

9.4. Insurance and Risk Management

Risk management, including liability and property insurance, is an area where skimping could have devastating effects. Your property management business should have insurance coverage that includes at least general liability, professional liability (Errors and Omissions coverage), and property insurance.

Additionally, state laws may oblige your business to hold workers' compensation insurance for your employees. Setting aside a reserve fund for unforeseen expenses or accidents may also be a smart tactic to consider.

In summary, launching your own property management business necessitates comprehensive diligence in understanding the legal landscape and regulatory requirements. An investment in conscientious planning and research now will undoubtedly bring significant return in avoiding potentially costly and damaging legal disputes in the future.

Moreover, by demonstrating a commitment to transparency, fairness, and legality, you fortify your reputation in the industry as a reliable, professional, and ethical business, thus setting a firm foundation for successful long-term relationships with both property owners and tenants alike.

Chapter 10. Growth Strategies: Scaling Your Property Management Business

Taking the first crucial step into property management is indeed a significant achievement, but to ensure consistent growth and profitability, devising and implementing proper growth strategies are crucial. They provide direction, helping to streamline and focus your business activities.

10.1. Understand Your Market

This involves researching and keeping updated about your local real estate conditions. Regularly analyze market trends, like rental rates and property prices. Understanding your competition and their strategies is also part of this process. By identifying your competitor's strengths and weaknesses, you can spot opportunities to outperform them.

10.2. Diversify Your Property Portfolio

Diversification is a key strategy to shield your business from the volatilities of the market. This involves managing a mix of different types of properties, including commercial, residential, and industrial properties. Each type of property has unique features, advantages, and disadvantages. By diversifying your portfolio, you can ensure a steady flow of income, even when one segment of the real estate market is not performing well.

10.3. Prioritize Customer Satisfaction

The key to a successful property management business is satisfying and retaining tenants. Ensure that you are providing prompt and quality service to your tenants. This can be through regular maintenance, prompt responses to queries and complaints, and providing comfort amenities. Satisfied tenants are more likely to extend their lease and recommend your service to others.

10.4. Leverage Technology

Technology plays an important role in streamlining operations and boosting efficiency. From property and tenant management software to virtual reality for property tours, there are technological solutions for nearly every aspect of the property management business. Use these tools to enhance your service offerings and optimize operational efficiency.

10.5. Networking and Partnerships

In real estate, it's not just about what you know, but also who you know. Establishing robust relationships can open doors to new opportunities and partnerships. Network with property owners, real estate agents, contractors, legal advisors, and other real estate professionals. Attending industry events and being active in local real estate community discussions can vastly aid in forming meaningful connections.

10.6. Improve Your Financial Management

Effective financial management is crucial for commercial success. Understand your revenue streams and main areas of expenditure. Have a clear budget and adhere to it, leaving some wiggle room for unexpected costs. Use accounting software to track income and expenses regularly and accurately. Also, ensuring that all financial regulatory and legal protocols are adhered to is essential.

10.7. Additional Services

Offering additional services can be critical in setting your business apart from the competition. These might include property maintenance services, renovation and refurbishment services, or legal advisory services related to property ownership and rental. These additional services not only provide more value to your clients, but also become additional revenue streams for your business.

10.8. Employee Training

Your employees are the face of your business and play a crucial role in maintaining client relationships. Regular training programs and workshops ensure they are updated with the latest trends and best practices in the industry. This invests in their skill development, hence ultimately benefiting your business.

10.9. Strategic Advertising and Marketing

Marketing and branding play vital roles in enhancing your business's visibility and attracting new clients. Use both offline and online platforms for advertising. A well-optimized website, engaging social media presence, and efficient email marketing can attract potential clients and retain existing ones.

10.10. Metrics and Performance Indicators

Regularly evaluate your business performance using Key Performance Indicators (KPIs) and metrics. These metrics can include average length of tenant stay, vacancy rates, operation expenses, and return on investment. This helps you understand the areas where you are performing well and the ones where improvement is needed.

Remember, successful growth in property management does not happen overnight. It requires consistent effort, steady progress, and a strategic approach to risk management. Embracing new technologies, nurturing relationships, diversifying your portfolio, all while putting your customers at the center of your business, will ensure you're well on your way to building a robust and prosperous property management empire.

Chapter 11. The Investor's Mindset: Time Management and Crisis Handling

Understanding an investor's mindset starts with acknowledging the fundamental principles that guide their actions. The highly successful investor realizes that time is a precious commodity and handles it with precision. Additionally, they proactively manage any form of crisis that may arise, often honing these skills through years of experience. In this chapter, we are going to take an in-depth dive into time management and crisis management, two pivotal aspects that hold the key to an investor's success.

11.1. Time is Money – Mastering the Art of Property Management Efficiency

One of the often-underemphasized aspects of property management is time management. As a property manager, your time is one of your most valuable assets. Proper time management helps streamline tasks, heighten productivity and ultimately increase your ROI.

Time management ranges from prioritizing tasks, utilizing technology for automation, delegating responsibilities, and setting achievable deadlines. All these alleviate the stress associated with juggling multiple tasks simultaneously.

` === Prioritizing Tasks

In property management, requests and tasks come at a fast pace, with various levels of urgency and importance. Utilizing the "Eisenhower Matrix," a grid separating tasks based on their urgency and importance, aids in categorizing these tasks and deciding on which ones need immediate attention.

The matrix consists of four quadrants:

- Quadrant 1: Important and urgent tasks. Examples include emergencies, repairs, appraisal meetings.
- Quadrant 2: Important but not urgent tasks. Examples include planning and strategizing, seeking investments, networking.
- Quadrant 3: Not important but urgent tasks. Examples include scheduling meetings, non-essential communication.
- Quadrant 4: Not important and not urgent tasks. Examples include miscellaneous non-consequential tasks.

Using the matrix, you'll be able to focus on the important elements of your day and effectively delegate or defer the rest.

` === Technology to the Rescue

Property management software solutions available today allow streamlining of daily operations like tenant applications, interviews, background checks, maintenance, rent collection, and financial reporting. Leverage them to scale faster and manage time more effectively.

` === Delegating Responsibilities

The secret to rapidly scaling your property management business is a well-organized, efficient team. Assign tasks based on individual skill sets. Effective delegation fosters creativity and allows you to focus on the more high-priority tasks.

` === Setting Achievable Deadlines

Create realistic and achievable schedules and deadlines. Setting unattainable deadlines can lead to burnout and undermine your team's morale.

Maintaining a clear calendar, breaking down larger projects into smaller, manageable tasks, and setting dedicated time for essential work are a few ways to create achievable timelines.

11.2. Crisis Management – Handling and Avoiding Common Pitfalls

Despite careful planning and proactive measures, crises are inevitable in property management. The key is in developing a proactive and efficient crisis management plan, encapsulating a structured approach for handling emergencies, potential crises, and unforeseen situations.

` === Developing a Crisis Management Plan

Having a crisis management plan helps prepare for worst-case scenarios. A good plan should incorporate a comprehensive crisis assessment, designating tasks to team members, establishing communication guidelines, and steps for recovery.

` === Regular Property Maintenance and Inspections

Regular property inspection and maintenance help identify potential issues before they escalate into full-blown crises. Include a regular schedule for preventive maintenance checks on essential aspects like plumbing, electrical systems, fire safety equipment, and structural integrity.

` === Efficient Communication During Crises

An apt quote states, "The single biggest problem in communication is the illusion that it has taken place." Clear communication is vital during adversity. Make sure everyone involved knows what's happening, what steps are being taken, and how it affects them.

` === Crisis Recovery and Follow-up

Post-crisis, it's crucial to conduct a post-mortem, examining what transpired, how it was resolved, and the steps needed to ensure it doesn't happen again.

In conclusion, mastering time management and crisis management is integral to operational success in the property management business. Striking a balance between these two aspects marks the difference between surviving and thriving in the dynamic, fast-paced world of property management. Make these elements your allies, and they'll significantly help propel your business towards its destined success.

www.ingramcontent.com/pod-product-compliance
Lightning Source LLC
Chambersburg PA
CBHW072222290526
45794CB00007B/2852